Year **1**

God Is Faithful

STUDENT GUIDE

> Forever, O LORD, Your word is settled in heaven. Your faithfulness endures to all generations; You established the earth, and it abides.—Psalm 119:89–90

GOD'S WORD FOR ALL GENERATIONS

Answers
BIBLE CURRICULUM

Answers Bible Curriculum

Year 1 • Quarter 3 • Adult Student

Second Edition

For more information write:
Answers in Genesis
PO Box 510
Hebron, KY 41048

Printed in China.

Contents

Genesis 1–11 have been the most-attacked chapters in all of Scripture. Creation in six days, the Fall of man, the global Flood, the Tower of Babel—all these events are dismissed by secularists (and some Christians) as nothing but myth.

Over the next 13 weeks we will be continuing our look at these important and foundational chapters. We'll answer questions such as: Did the Flood of Noah's day cover the entire earth? Was the Ark large enough to house all the animals onboard? Can the incident at the Tower of Babel be believed?

We'll also begin to look at Abraham—the amazing promises God made to him as well as his place as the father of the nation of Israel (and the father of all true believers). And we will see, once again, that the Bible can be trusted, and that what we see in God's world confirms what we read in God's Word.

We encourage you to read the Prepare to Learn section before class each week. This will provide important background information so that you will get more from each lesson.

For more information and links to online articles and videos, be sure to visit the Online Resource Page at www. AnswersBibleCurriculum.com.

Catastrophe: The Flood

1

Key Passages

- Genesis 6:5–7:1; 2 Peter 2:4–5; Hebrews 11:7

What You Will Learn

- How sin grieves God and leads to judgment.
- The source of Noah's righteousness.

Lesson Overview

The third C of Catastrophe begins when God calls Noah out from a world filled with violence and corruption. God intended to judge the sin of the world by wiping out mankind. But Noah found grace in God's eyes and was called to reestablish the population after the Flood.

Memory Verse

2 Peter 2:5 And [God] did not spare the ancient world, but saved Noah, one of eight people, a preacher of righteousness, bringing in the flood on the world of the ungodly.

📖 Prepare to Learn

SCRIPTURAL BACKGROUND

The account of Noah begins in Genesis 6. Genesis 6:5–6 says that God saw the wickedness of man and that He was grieved and sorry that He had made man. Scripture describes the situation at the time: "wickedness of man was great," "evil thoughts continually" (Genesis 6:5), "corrupt" (Genesis 6:11–12), "filled with violence" (Genesis 6:11, 6:13).

Hebrews 11:7 tells us that by faith, Noah was divinely warned of things not yet seen. He was warned by God of the coming destruction, and it was Noah's faith that led to his obedience and the salvation of his family. Because Noah is described as a "preacher of righteousness" (2 Peter 2:5), we can imagine that he spent his time while building the Ark trying to persuade the people to be righteous and warning them of God's coming judgment. However, only Noah's family believed and joined him in the Ark. Noah was a "just man" (Genesis 6:9), he "walked with God" (Genesis 6:9), and it was by faith that he believed, obeyed, and was saved (Hebrews 11:7).

God shows in this account that He does judge all sin. The Flood wiped out the entire population and was a bitter judgment. But, as God saved Noah and his family in the Ark, He has also shown us His mercy and grace by providing salvation from our sins through His own Son, Jesus Christ.

APOLOGETICS BACKGROUND

Looking at the full counsel of the Word of God we see that several other biblical writers were inspired by the Holy Spirit to confirm the historical account of Noah and the Flood. It was more than 1,700 years after the Flood that the prophet Ezekiel mentioned Noah (Ezekiel 14:14, 14:20). And about 2,400 years after Noah lived, Jesus Christ referred to him as He described His return and coming judgment (Matthew 24:37–39).

The writer of Hebrews also confirmed Noah's existence when he included him in the "Hall of Faith" chapter, (Hebrews 11:7). Peter writes of both Noah and the Flood, again confirming that this watery judgment occurred just as we read in Genesis. Noah was a real person called by God during this amazing time in history.

In addition, the sheer size, dimensions, and directions given by God to Noah for building the Ark show that this vessel was seaworthy and able to withstand a year-long global Flood. In other words, the Ark itself confirms the Flood.

HISTORICAL BACKGROUND

A careful reading of Genesis confirms again God's precision in handing down the history of the universe. Noah was born 1,056 years after Creation (Genesis 5). He was 500 years old when he began to build the Ark. It could have taken up to 75 years for him to complete the project. It is a good practice to take special note of details when God so specifically gives them.

In the years following the Fall, mankind became more and more self-willed. They were filled with violence and the thoughts of their hearts were only evil continually. Because God hates sin, He had to judge the world. This judgment came via the worldwide Flood.

Here is the timeline of Noah and the Flood as gleaned from the book of Genesis:

- Year 0 – Creation
- 1056 – Noah born (Genesis 5)
- 1536 – Proclamation of judgment by God ("in 120 years earth will be destroyed")
- ~1581–1601 – God instructs Noah to build Ark and Noah begins building and preaching
- 1656 – God instructs Noah to prepare to enter Ark; Noah enters and God shuts the door; the Flood begins
- 40 days – Rains fall and fountains of deep break open
- 110 days – Water covers earth, begins to recede, Ark rests on mountain
- 74 days – Waters continue to decrease, tops of mountains seen
- 40 days – Noah sends out a raven, which does not return
- 7 days – Noah sends out a dove, which returns
- 7 days – Noah sends out a dove, which returns with olive branch
- 7 days – Noah sends out a dove, which does not return
- 29 days – Noah removes the cover from Ark
- 56 days – Noah and his family leave Ark
- 1657 – The Flood is over; God instructs Noah to leave Ark

Noah and his family were on the Ark for 371 days.

For more information on this topic, go to the Online Resource Page.

 **Studying God's Word**

What made Noah righteous?

Take notes as you study the following passages.

Genesis 6:5–7:1

2 Peter 2:4–5

Hebrews 11:7

 Corruption and Righteousness

Complete the Corruption and Righteousness activity following your teacher's instructions.

God's Word in the Real World

1. Having talked about the source of Noah's righteousness, how can you apply that to yourself?

2. What is the importance of faith as we consider the call of Noah and the call God has for each of our lives?

3. People often claim that God is cruel to have wiped out every person on the face of the earth in the Flood. How would you use the texts we have discussed today to help them understand that God's actions were just?

4. Noah is described as a preacher of righteousness to an ungodly world. Is our situation any different from his? How should we live in light of this truth?

5. Why is it important to recognize that our righteousness does not come from us, but is found in Christ alone?

 **Prayer Requests**

2

God Saves Noah

Key Passage

- Genesis 6:1–9:19

What You Will Learn

- What was destroyed and preserved in the Flood.
- The timing of events surrounding the Flood.
- How the salvation of the Ark relates to salvation in Christ.

Lesson Overview

The account of the Flood is no fairy tale, but a detailed record of how a holy God punished an ungodly world for its sinfulness. Noah and his family alone escaped God's wrath as they obeyed God and boarded the Ark. The Ark is a picture of salvation in Christ—a refuge for everyone who will take shelter in Him.

Memory Verse

2 Peter 2:5 And [God] did not spare the ancient world, but saved Noah, one of eight people, a preacher of righteousness, bringing in the flood on the world of the ungodly.

SCRIPTURAL BACKGROUND

Even though Noah was a "preacher of righteousness," calling people to repent for nearly 75 years, no one but his family came into the Ark with him. The people who heard Noah's message of imminent judgment refused to believe. When the Flood came, Noah and his family were safe in the Ark, but every other person and air-breathing, land-dwelling animal on the earth was destroyed: all flesh died that moved on the earth (Genesis 7:21), every man (Genesis 7:21), all in whose nostrils was the breath of the spirit of life (Genesis 7:22), all that was on the dry land died (Genesis 7:22). So He destroyed all living things (Genesis 7:23); they were destroyed from the earth (Genesis 7:23); only Noah and those who were with him in the Ark remained alive (Genesis 7:23). God was faithful to His promise that He would provide and protect in the midst of this severe judgment (Genesis 6:18).

God revealed His patience with the people of Noah's day by allowing them time to repent, but because of His nature—His holiness and justice—He finally had to punish the wicked and those who were suppressing the truth. "For the wrath of God is revealed from heaven against all ungodliness and unrighteousness of men, who suppress the truth in unrighteousness" (Romans 1:18).

While the rest of the world was being destroyed outside, Noah and his family were safe in the Ark. God mercifully rewarded Noah's faith and obedience by saving him and his family from the Flood. God continues to demonstrate that mercy to all of us through Jesus Christ. We can think of the Ark as an example of how we can be saved from God's judgment on our sin. Just as Noah entered the door of the Ark to be saved, so we are saved if we repent, turn from our sins, and in faith and obedience trust Jesus Christ for forgiveness and salvation.

APOLOGETICS BACKGROUND

The Bible is very specific about the timeline of the Flood. Although biblical skeptics arbitrarily dismiss this account as pure mythology, Christians stand on the Word of God, our Creator who was there, rather than the opinions of fallible men who were not.

The Flood came in the six hundredth year of Noah's life, in the second month, on the seventeenth day of the month. Scripture records that on that day all the fountains of the great deep burst open (Genesis 7:11). And the waters prevailed upon the earth one hundred and fifty days

(Genesis 7:24). As we examine the Flood account in Genesis 6–8, we can determine the overall progression of the year-long global Flood. The table below summarizes the timing of the Flood based on Scripture.

Timeline of the Flood	Description	Bible reference
Day 0	The fountains of the great deep broke apart and the windows of heaven were opened; it began to rain.	Genesis 7:11
Day 150 (Includes the 40 days and nights in Genesis 7:12)	The water rose to its highest level (covering the whole earth) sometime between the 40th and 150th day. On the 150th day, the springs of the great deep were shut off, the rain from above ceased, and the water began continually receding. The Ark rested on the mountains of Ararat.	Genesis 7:11–12 Genesis 7:17–20 Genesis 7:24–8:5
Day 224	The tops of the mountains became visible on the first day of the tenth month.	Genesis 8:5
Day 264	After 40 more days, Noah sent out a raven.	Genesis 8:6–7
Day 271	After seven days the dove was sent out after the raven. It had no resting place and returned to Noah. * Note: Gen. 8:10 says, "After another seven days" or "He waited seven more days." In the Hebrew this implies that there was a previous period of seven days, which must be between the raven and first dove, though there is some debate on this.	Genesis 8:8–9
Day 278	After seven more days, Noah sent out the dove again. It returned again but this time with an olive leaf in its beak.	Genesis 8:10–11
Day 285	After seven more days, Noah sent out the dove again, and it did not return.	Genesis 8:12
Day 314	Noah removed the cover of the Ark on the first day of the first month. The surface of the earth was dried up and Noah could verify this to the extent of what he could see.	Genesis 8:13
Day 371	The earth was dry and God commanded Noah's family and the animals to come out of the Ark.	Genesis 8:14–17

The Flood was a real event, specifically recorded in God's Word. It was a catastrophic judgment by God on man's wickedness that lasted over one year.

HISTORICAL BACKGROUND

Because the Bible is the true history book of the universe you can be confident that the Flood was a real event—and it occurred just as the Bible tells us. Many people wonder how Noah could have possibly built an Ark of this proportion, even in 75 years! Although the biblical record is not specific about this, we do know a few things.

When God created Adam, he was perfect and perfectly intelligent. Noah and the people of his day were fairly recent descendants of Adam—probably maintaining much of the intelligence God originally blessed man with.

Building the Ark was a huge task—one that had never been accomplished before. And, although the Bible doesn't record much information about the world before the Flood, we know the people of this time were very intelligent. Genesis gives us insight into these folks and what they were capable of. For instance, they built cities (Genesis 4:17), raised and cared for livestock (Genesis 4:20), made and played musical instruments (Genesis 4:21), and were metalworkers in bronze and iron (Genesis 4:22).

Many people dismiss this historical event as impossible—both the Flood and the Ark that survived it—but with God's guidance, Noah's faith, and the intelligence of man, it was accomplished in God's timing according to God's purpose.

For more information on this topic, see the Online Resource Page.

 ## Studying God's Word

How do fairy tales begin?

Take notes as you study the following passages.

Genesis 6:1–9:19

1 Peter 3:20

2 Peter 2:5

Hebrews 11:7

 ## Christ, Our Ark

Complete the Christ, Our Ark worksheet.

God's Word in the Real World

1. How would you use the text of this passage to respond to someone who thought this account was just a mythical story about a man and a boat?

2. Many people have a Noah's Ark theme for their nursery or children's play area. What is the real message of the Flood and is that really fitting for a nursery?

3. What can we learn about God's character by comparing the salvation of the Ark and the salvation in Christ?

4. How should we approach God knowing that He is holy and will judge mankind for its sinfulness?

5. We see Noah as an example of faith and obedience in the face of many unknowns. What unknowns are you facing in your life, and how can you walk in obedience to God through those unknowns? What can you expect from God as you do that?

 # Prayer Requests

3
Was the Flood Global?

Key Passages

*   Genesis 6–9; Luke 17:26–30; 2 Peter 2:5

What You Will Learn

*   Several points that confirm the global Flood—both from God's Word and from human history.

*   The significance and sign of the covenant that God made with mankind after the Flood.

*   How the local and global explanations for the Flood compare.

Lesson Overview

The fact that the Genesis Flood was global is very clear from the language of the text. Some reject this understanding, teaching that the Flood was a local event. The rainbow covenant and flood legends from around the world confirm the global nature of the Flood.

Memory Verse

2 Peter 2:5 And [God] did not spare the ancient world, but saved Noah, one of eight people, a preacher of righteousness, bringing in the flood on the world of the ungodly.

📖 Prepare to Learn

SCRIPTURAL BACKGROUND

We know that the Flood of Noah's day was global. However, this is a fact that is being denied frequently by secularists and some Christians. A clear look at Scripture and a steadfast commitment to biblical authority show us the truth.

A simple reading of Genesis 7:19–20 will put an end to the discussion. "And the waters prevailed exceedingly on the earth, and all the high hills under the whole heaven were covered. The waters prevailed fifteen cubits upward, and the mountains were covered." This does not mean that the Flood was merely 15 cubits deep—verse 20 explains that the Flood "prevailed" over the tops of the highest mountains to a depth of 15 cubits. (A cubit was a standard means of measurement at the time, which was determined by measuring from the elbow to the tip of the finger—generally resulting in 18 to 20 inches. Fifteen cubits may have been about 22 feet.) These facts about the Flood cannot be reconciled with the idea of a local flood. You cannot have a mountain-covering local flood that lasts over a year.

Then Genesis 7:21 reiterates the total destruction of this Flood on all the earth. "And all flesh died that moved on the earth: birds and cattle and beasts and every creeping thing that creeps on the earth, and every man."

We learn in Genesis 9:11–17 that the rainbow was the sign that God used to promise He would never again flood the entire world: "the waters shall never again become a flood to destroy all flesh" (Genesis 9:15). If the Flood were not a global event, God would have repeatedly broken that promise whenever a local flood happened on earth after His promise to Noah.

As students of the Word of God we need to learn to use Scripture to interpret and confirm Scripture. In that light, let's take a look at a couple of New Testament passages that talk of this global Flood in definitive ways.

In warning of God's judgment on wickedness we see in 2 Peter 2:5 a reference to a global Flood that came upon the earth and spared only Noah and his family—"[God] did not spare the ancient world, but saved Noah, one of eight people, a preacher of righteousness, bringing in the flood on the world of the ungodly."

Jesus Christ Himself confirmed that He believed the Flood killed every person not on the Ark. He referred to this catastrophic Flood as He prepared His disciples for the coming of the Son of Man: "And as it was in the days of Noah, so it will be also in the days of the Son of Man. They ate, they drank, they married wives, they were given in marriage, until the day that Noah entered the ark, and the flood came and destroyed them all" (Luke 17:26–27). This reference to Noah is repeated in Matthew 24:37–39.

In summary, the following are reasons to be confident that the Bible is clear—the Flood of Noah's day was global.

- Confirmation of Scripture with Scripture—Jesus Christ and others in the New Testament referring to the Flood.

- The language used in Genesis 7:17–24 describes the Flood as global. For example, "all the high hills under the whole heaven were covered, "all flesh died that moved on the earth," "the waters prevailed on the earth," etc.

- The depth and duration of the Flood—15 cubits above the mountains; 371 days total.

- The rainbow covenant.

APOLOGETICS BACKGROUND

Because of the wide belief in evolutionary history, many people deny that Noah's Flood was a global catastrophe. They rely on the secular interpretation of geologic formations on the earth as truth. They look to man's ideas first to interpret rock layers, rather than looking to God's Word as the ultimate authority. It is true that the geological processes we see today are slow. But this in no way infers that this is the way it has *always* been.

Again, a clear reading of Genesis, as mentioned above, gives us an understanding of how catastrophic this Flood was. The depth of the water, the destruction recorded in Scripture, and the duration of the Flood are a few of the scriptural evidences given to us by God.

But what would we expect to see on the earth if this Flood were real? Wouldn't we expect to find billions of dead things buried in rock layers laid down by water all over the earth? Yes! And that *is* what we find. Take a look below at some evidences that confirm the reality of a global Flood.

1. Fossils of sea creatures atop high mountains. The global Flood covered the "high hills" Genesis says. At the end of the Flood, the rapidly moving continental plates rammed into each other, causing the formation of mountains. The floodwaters did not rise to cover present-day Mt. Everest, for example. Rather, Mt. Everest was formed after the layers were deposited.

2. The sheer existence of the fossil record including fossil "graveyards"—exhibiting the rapid burial of plants and animals. These animals had to have been buried quickly or they would have rotted away, leaving no evidence to confirm this massive Flood.

3. Rock layers that have been discovered to stretch across continents—some with similar features that can be traced for thousands of miles. These layers indicate a rapid deposition that can be explained by the water devastation described in Genesis.

4. Rock layers that are "folded" or bent with no evidence of fracturing or breaking. These folds could only have been formed if these layers were laid down rapidly over one another while still wet and pliable—before solidifying into rock—discounting the idea that this would have taken millions of years.

Another important fact to remember when defending the reality of a global Flood is that the Bible seems to indicate that the landmasses of the earth were once all connected. In Genesis 1:9 we read, "Then God said, 'Let the waters under the heavens be gathered together into one place, and let the dry land appear'; and it was so."

You may have heard of *plate tectonics*. This term refers to the moving of the earth's plates. These movements are still observed today, though they are very slow. This observation has led secular scientists to suggest that the earth is billions of years old. However, many creationists believe that the breaking apart of the earth's surface into the continents we know today is best understood in terms of the Flood of Noah's day—a theory called *catastrophic plate tectonics*. This rapid movement of the plates would have been triggered when "all the fountains of the great deep were broken up" (Genesis 7:11).

More than all the physical evidence we can provide, Jesus Christ, our Creator, spoke of the Flood as real, literal history, and the words recorded in Genesis by God Himself cannot be disputed. Every word of His is true, and we are not to add to His words lest we be found liars (Proverbs 30:5–6).

HISTORICAL BACKGROUND

God's Word is the history book of the universe from beginning to end, and this global Flood is a major part of that history.

The only way we could know for sure whether this event really occurred and whether it was global or local is if there were an eyewitness record of what happened. And there is! The God of history moved men by His Spirit to write His Word. In God's Word, we are told that Noah's Flood was a real event. The Flood lasted for 371 days and covered all the high hills under the whole heaven (Genesis 7:19).

But there is other information available to us. Did you know that stories about a worldwide Flood are found in historic records all over the world? There have been more than 200 of these stories documented, in practically all nations, from ancient Babylon onward. And they all have common threads weaving throughout them—mimicking the Flood of Noah. This cannot be discounted as "coincidence." For if there never were a global Flood, where would these stories have come from?

Another historical verification lies in the writings of a well-known and respected first-century Jewish historian named Josephus. This man served as a governor of Galilee, fought against Rome in the first century, and was eventually captured. He was imprisoned in Rome and was ordered to write a history of the Jewish nation. In *The Revised Works of Josephus*, he writes, "When God gave the signal, and it began to rain, the water poured down forty entire days, till it became fifteen cubits higher than the earth; which was the reason why there was no greater number preserved, since they had no place to flee to."

This statement from the famous historian confirms God's Word, but also gives evidence that the Jewish population in the first century believed the Flood to be global and a real event.

For more on this topic, see the Online Resource Page.

 ## Studying God's Word

Why do most cultures around the globe have a legend of a global flood?

Take notes as you study the following passages.

Genesis 6:7, 6:11–13, 6:17; 7:4, 7:11–12, 7:17–24; 8:1–2

2 Peter 2:5

Luke 17:26–30

Genesis 9:8–17

 Flood Legends

Complete the Flood Legends worksheet in pairs or small groups.

 God's Word in the Real World

1. As you interact with people, what is the most likely objection to the Flood account from Genesis?

2. As we talk with unbelievers, should we use the various flood legends from around the world to prove that the biblical Flood really happened?

3. What elements of the text of Genesis 6–9 could you use to point someone to the global nature of the Flood?

4. When talking with a fellow believer who believes (or has been taught) that the Flood was only a local event, how would you approach correcting their understanding?

5. Do you think a Noah's Ark/rainbow theme is appropriate for a nursery?

6. How can you use a rainbow flag or pin someone is wearing to begin a conversation about the gospel?

7. How can we connect the Flood to the gospel?

8. How does Genesis 6–9 point to Christ?

Prayer Requests

4
How Large Was the Ark?

Key Passage

- Genesis 6:13–22

What You Will Learn

- How typical representations of the Ark compare to the biblical description.

- The kinds of animals that were taken on the Ark.

Lesson Overview

The size of the Ark and the number of animals on board are sources of constant attack from skeptics of the Bible's account. Despite claims to the contrary, the Ark was a massive vessel that was more than able to hold the kinds of animals that God preserved on board.

Memory Verse

2 Peter 2:5 And [God] did not spare the ancient world, but saved Noah, one of eight people, a preacher of righteousness, bringing in the flood on the world of the ungodly.

📖 Prepare to Learn

SCRIPTURAL BACKGROUND

The account of Noah and the Ark is often taken as a mere fairytale. The Bible, however, is the true history book of the universe, and in that light we can have confidence in what it says about the Ark. Scripture reveals the basic dimensions of Noah's Ark—the length, width, and height. According to God's Word, it was massive—300 cubits long, 50 cubits wide, and 30 cubits high (approximately 510 feet long, 85 feet wide, and 51 feet high based on a cubit of 20.4 inches). This is not like the whimsical drawings that depict the Ark as an overgrown houseboat with giraffes and other animals hanging on and sticking out the top.

In addition to its size, God gave other specific information about the Ark in Genesis 6:14–16. His instructions to Noah include the type of wood—gopherwood; a pitch coating—cover it inside and outside with pitch; a window—you shall make a window for the Ark, and you shall finish it to a cubit from above; three decks—make it with lower, second, and third decks; and a door—set the door of the Ark in its side. The specificity in Scripture gives us confidence that this was, in fact, a ship ordained by God to withstand the watery judgment soon to cover the entire earth.

However, a detailed design of the ship's hull is not given.

Biblical creationists have historically depicted the Ark as a simple rectangular box. You will notice that the Ark shown in *Answers Bible Curriculum* goes beyond that rectangular configuration. This particular model was considered after much study and the determination that the Ark had to have been equipped to handle rough seas. This design was made by a mechanical engineer who studied the Flood and the Ark for nearly 13 years before rendering this design.

The rough seas confronting the Ark during the Flood are alluded to in Scripture.

- Genesis 6:15—The Ark had the proportions of a seagoing vessel built for waves.

- Genesis 7:19—A mountain-covering, global Flood would not be dead calm.

- Genesis 7:18—The Ark moved about on the surface of the waters.

- Genesis 8:1—God made a wind to pass over the earth.

- Psalm 104:8 (NAS)—The earth's landmasses were shifting during the Flood. This would cause tremendous turbulence in the waters as they receded.

By wearing our biblical glasses, considering the full counsel of God's Word, and in view of historical information, we can be certain that the Ark commissioned by God Himself was large enough to withstand a global Flood and had room for all the animals God intended to be saved.

APOLOGETICS BACKGROUND

For centuries scoffers have mocked the account of Noah and the Flood by arguing that it would have been impossible for the Ark to hold two of every species of animal. This supposition leads to the conclusion that the Flood account was not inspired by God—thus casting doubt on all of God's Word.

There are some serious misconceptions here that need to be clarified. First of all, God did not send representatives of all the "species" of animals to Noah—but rather the "kinds" of animals (Genesis 8:19). For example, Noah would not have had two African elephants, two Asian elephants, along with two mastodons, two mammoths, and two stegodons (these last three are now extinct). He would have only needed two representatives of the elephant kind. Then after the Flood, when the animals spread out over all the earth, different species resulted from the tremendous amount of information God had designed into the genes of each of these animals, as they adapted to their environments. Noah didn't need the number of

animals many people think he did. There was plenty of room!

People think that most land animals are very large like elephants and giraffes. But actually only about 11% of land animals are larger than a sheep. So the average size of the animals on the Ark would have been smaller than the size of a sheep.

Something else we often hear is that there is no way all the dinosaurs could have fit on the Ark. But though there are about 700 names of dinosaurs, all of them fall into approximately 50 different kinds of dinosaurs. And not all dinosaurs were huge like the brachiosaurus—many were much smaller. And even these larger animals were probably young when they boarded the Ark, thus taking up less room and still having their reproductive lives ahead of them as they left the Ark to be fruitful and multiply and fill the earth.

The study of created kinds, called *baraminology*, is dependent on biblical truth. One of the tenets of this science is that the various kinds created by God do not interbreed with other kinds. Genesis clearly states that animals reproduce after their kind. And this is what real science shows—dogs produce dogs, cats produce cats, horses produce horses, etc. Secular scientists, however, continue to defend their belief that all life has common ancestry even though observable science has never recorded any "kind" changing into another "kind."

As Christians, we must continue to stand on the authority of God's Word, answering questions using our biblical glasses. As we continue to do that, our confidence in the infallibility of the Word of God can only strengthen.

HISTORICAL BACKGROUND

It is difficult to speak historically about Noah's Ark. The only true account we have of it is given through God in the book of Genesis. However, as discussed in a previous lesson (Lesson 3, "Was the Flood Global?"), we have record of more than 200 stories of a global Flood from all around the world. Native Americans, Hawaiians, Australian Aborigines, Inuit, and more—all have flood stories passed down from their ancestors that sound a lot like Noah's Flood as recorded in Genesis.

We can also pursue history when researching the Ark's size, shape, and construction. Some say no wooden ship of this size would hold together. One of the greatest challenges to the construction of large wooden ships is finding a way to lay planks around the outside that will ensure little or no leaking. Recently, however, marine archaeologists have discovered a method of planking used on ancient Greek ships that had been lost for centuries. This discovery raises the idea that this may have been the method handed down for years—even from Noah's day!

It is important to remember that we have the history book of the universe—the Bible. And we have an eyewitness to the account of Noah's Flood and the judgment it brought. That eyewitness is God, our Creator; the source is the Bible, His infallible Word.

For much more information on this topic, go to the Online Resource Page.

 Studying God's Word

What do pictures of Noah's Ark typically look like?

 Ark Facts

Complete the Ark Facts worksheet as you work through the lesson.

Take notes as you study the following passages.

Genesis 6:13–16

Genesis 6:17–22

God's Word in the Real World

1. What misconceptions about the Ark did you have corrected from this discussion?

2. What types of doubts about the size of the Ark have you heard from others? How can you respond to those objections in light of what you have learned today?

3. How might the pictures of an overloaded, miniature Ark influence people's view of the accounts in Scripture?

4. What questions have been raised by this lesson, and what can you do to understand these issues better?

Prayer Requests

5
Reshaping the Earth

Key Passages

- Genesis 1:9–10, 7:10–16, 8:1–7; Psalm 104:6–9

What You Will Learn

- The source of the water for the Flood.
- How the earth's surface changed during the Flood.
- How the fossils in the earth's rock layers relate to the Flood.

Lesson Overview

The Bible describes the Flood as a global event that reshaped the surface of the earth. The waters from under the earth flooded the entire surface of the earth as the continents broke apart. As the floodwaters receded, the mountains rose, and the valleys sank to receive the water. The billions of dead things that were buried by the floodwaters are evident as fossils in the rock layers today.

Memory Verse

2 Peter 2:5 And [God] did not spare the ancient world, but saved Noah, one of eight people, a preacher of righteousness, bringing in the flood on the world of the ungodly.

📖 Prepare to Learn

SCRIPTURAL BACKGROUND

The Bible describes Noah's Flood as a globe-covering event with water moving about. Scripture describes the water sources and also where the water went as it began to recede. There is not a lot of detail given in Scripture about the pre-Flood world, but there are many clues that we can use to piece together how the earth changed during the Flood.

Genesis 1:9–13 describes Day Three of Creation. Verse 9 seems to suggest that there was originally one land mass. If the waters were gathered together in one place and the land appears out of that, it makes sense that there was one land mass surrounded by water. It is this land that Genesis 7 describes as being covered by floodwaters. The high hills may not have been as tall as the mountains we have today. Covering them would not have required the same amount of water as would be required today.

The source of the water for the Flood is described from Scripture. First, we read of the "fountains of the great deep" that broke open to release water. Most understand these to be some sort of water source within the earth. As the earth's crust cracked open, sea water would have come into contact with the extremely hot magma that erupted from inside the earth. As the magma was released and

cooled, it would have caused great jets of steam to blast into the atmosphere, carrying sea water with it. Some of this steam would have condensed to form clouds, but it would have been the sea water carried aloft that was the main source of the rain described as coming from the "windows of heaven." Today, there is much water found under the ground in cracks and in porous rocks (reservoirs or aquifers) in the earth's crust, left there after the receding of the floodwaters.

Others have suggested that there may have been a canopy of water above the earth (Genesis 1:6) that supplied the rain. This idea presents more challenges than it solves and is not a necessary conclusion from the text. The heaviest rain continued for forty days, and on day 150 the sources of the water were shut up. God sent a wind, and the Ark came to rest on mountains that were being lifted up from under the floodwaters due to the dramatic movements of the earth's crust that continued until the end of the Flood 221 days later.

Psalm 104 describes a portion of the events of the Flood in verses 6–9. Some versions seem to indicate that the waters are the subject of verse 8, but the Hebrew seems to best support the ESV translation: "The mountains rose, the valleys sank down to the place that you appointed for them." Many contend that this section is a reference to Day Three of the Creation Week. Verse 9, however, seems to refute this idea since the waters are not to "return to cover the earth." This could not be about the Creation because the waters did indeed cover the earth again during the Flood. Proponents of a local Flood point to this verse to support their claim that the Flood was not global.

As the continents continued to shift and collide, mountains were pushed up and valleys sank down. The floodwaters retreated from the earth, causing massive erosional features. The new oceans were filled, and the land eventually dried, allowing plants to grow again. The landmass and sea that had existed before the Flood no longer existed—everything had been reshaped.

As we develop scientific models based on what the Bible reveals, we must take care not to add ideas into the text. We know that the Flood was global and that it destroyed all living things on the surface of the earth. That destruction is seen clearly in the billions of dead things buried in rock layers laid down by water across the globe.

APOLOGETICS BACKGROUND

Many people in the church today look to modern scientific explanations to explain the history of the earth more than they look to their Bibles. Rather than accepting the clear language of the text of Genesis 6–9, they seek to understand the rock layers, the fossils, and the legends of a global Flood in light of modern "wisdom." The secular understanding of rock layers that were deposited slowly over millions of years is imported into the Bible. As a result, many reject the idea that the Flood was global. Instead, they suggest that the Flood was a local event that was distorted over time into a global event. Others suggest that while the Flood was not global, it was "universal," meaning that it covered the area of the earth where mankind was living.

All of these positions depend on a modern understanding of science to interpret the biblical record of the Flood. This is the exact opposite way we should approach the Scriptures. God's Word should inform our understanding of what we observe in the world. We should interpret the rock layers that contain billions of dead things in light of the Flood account—not the other way around.

In this lesson we will look in greater detail at how the fossils and rock layers can be explained from the perspective of the Flood. The billions of dead things buried in rock layers laid down by water all over the earth are a testament to this globe-covering event.

If the Flood were not a global event, the details of Noah's adventure on the Ark would be absurd. If the Flood only covered the Mesopotamian region, as some would suggest, why didn't God just tell Noah to move? Why was it necessary to take all of the animals aboard when God could have directed them out of the area, just as He brought them to Noah? Has God broken His promise to never send another flood to destroy the earth, if the Flood was just local? All of these questions must be answered in light of what Scripture teaches, not what the secular scientists tell us.

Another important consideration comes from the study of cultures around the globe. Most cultures have some type of flood story. If we think about this from a biblical view, all of these cultures were founded as people were scattered from Babel about 100 years after the Flood. As they scattered, they carried the account of the Flood with them. Over time, the account turned into various stories. People's names are changed, the details are lost, and the focus shifts from the one true God, but many similarities remain.

Hawaiians have a flood story that tells of a time when, long after the death of the first man, the world became a wicked, terrible place. Only one good man was left, and his name was Nu'u. He made a great canoe with a house on it and filled it with animals. In this story, the waters came up over all the earth and killed all the people; only Nu'u and his family were saved.

Another flood story is from China. It records that Fuhi, his wife, three sons, and three daughters escaped a great flood and were the only people alive on earth. After the great flood, they repopulated the world.

These legends, along with many others, confirm the biblical view of history. We rely first on the infallible record of Scripture that comes directly from God, but we also see these other evidences as great confirmations of what is recorded for us.

HISTORICAL BACKGROUND

Over time, there have been many different explanations for the fossilized creatures found in the rock layers. Giant fossilized bones have been imagined to be dragons and giants by various cultures around the world. In the early 1800s, fossilized bones were found in England and were popularized as giant reptiles that once dominated the earth. It was during this period that the fossils and rock layers were being reinterpreted apart from a biblical understanding.

Up to that point, Noah's Flood was generally the explanation for the dead creatures buried in the layers. Rather than a single, global event, scientists began to insist that the layers were better explained by many smaller floods that happened successively over long periods of time. Rather than rapid and catastrophic, they imagined slow and gradual processes. This was the birth of uniformitarianism—the idea that the present is the key to the past. Since new rocks are formed slowly today, they assumed that this is how it had always happened. They rejected the clear record of Scripture and interpreted the rock layers to mean that the world was very old.

In 1859, the year Darwin published his famous book, Antonio Snider proposed that the continents had been connected at one point in the past. He looked at the way the coastlines of the continents appear to fit and proposed that the continents had moved apart during the Flood. In 1915, a secular scientist suggested that the continents had drifted apart slowly. This idea was later embraced by many scientists as the ocean floors were explored, and it has become the common belief.

Rather than happening slowly over millions of years, models based on the Bible suggest that the continents moved apart very rapidly during the Flood—as Snider had proposed. While the details of such models are tested, it is important that we hold loosely to our scientific models and hold fast to the clear truths from Scripture.

For more information on this topic, see the Online Resource Page.

Studying God's Word

Can we identify the spot where the Garden of Eden was located?

Take notes as you study the following passages.

Genesis 7:10–16

Genesis 1:9–10

Rock Layers Video Notes

Take notes as you view the Rock Layers video.

Take notes as you study the following passage.

Psalm 104:6–9

 ## God's Word in the Real World

1. In light of all that we have studied in this lesson, and the Flood as a whole, do you expect yourself to know all the answers to every question a skeptic might ask you about the Flood?

2. What if you don't know the answer to someone's question related to the Flood and geologic features? How can you respond?

3. Why can we trust that the Flood was a real event that truly reshaped the earth?

4. How can an understanding of the Flood help us understand more about the character and nature of God?

5. How can you use questions about the Flood to share the gospel with others around you?

Prayer Requests

Confusion: Dispersion at Babel

6

Key Passages

- Genesis 10:8–12, 10:25, 11:1–9

What You Will Learn

- The sin that caused God to judge mankind by changing the people's language.

- How the confusion of languages scattered people over the whole world.

Lesson Overview

After the Flood, God commanded the people to spread across the globe, but they refused and assembled together in Shinar. There they sought to build a city and a tower to make a name for themselves. God judged their sin by confusing their languages, causing them to scatter.

Memory Verse

Acts 17:26–27 And He has made from one blood every nation of men to dwell on all the face of the earth, and has determined their preappointed times and the boundaries of their dwellings, so that they should seek the Lord, in the hope that they might grope for Him and find Him, though He is not far from each one of us.

📖 Prepare to Learn

SCRIPTURAL BACKGROUND

After the Flood was over, Noah and his family—eight people in all—left the Ark. All the tribes and nations on the earth today have come from these eight people. God gave Noah and his family very specific instructions in Genesis 9:1: "So God blessed Noah and his sons, and said to them: 'Be fruitful and multiply, and fill the earth.'" God repeated this same command again in Genesis 9:7: "As for you, be fruitful and multiply; bring forth abundantly in the earth and multiply in it." Noah had been commissioned by God to repopulate the earth. Noah and his family obeyed this command; however, the descendants of Noah disobeyed.

While Noah's descendants were dispersing to fill the earth, the people, possibly under the powerful Nimrod (Genesis 10:9–10), stopped at the plain of Shinar to live (Genesis 11:2). There they began to build a city (Genesis 11:4). These people were openly rebellious and disobedient to God. First, they disobeyed God's specific instructions to disperse across the earth (Genesis 9:1, 9:7). Second, they were prideful in their disobedience by coveting a name for themselves (Genesis 11:4). They were anxious to build a monument to themselves whose top is in the heavens, looking to gain fame in the land among the people while disobeying the holy God.

This prideful attitude of blatant disobedience angered the Lord—as does all disobedience to Him. He came down to them and confused their language so they would not understand one another's speech (Genesis 11:7). Thus, these wicked people were scattered across the land, there was no longer a common language, and the building of the Tower of Babel ceased (Genesis 11:8–9). God's purpose to fill the earth was accomplished.

APOLOGETICS BACKGROUND

Christians are often faced with questions concerning how the world's history fits in with the biblical timeline. An example of this relates to the Tower of Babel. The secular world is continually making archaeological finds that supposedly pre-date the Flood. Be on the lookout for this. It is contradictory to what we know God's Word tells us.

For example, secular historians date the first civilizations around 8000–10000 BC, with Egyptian civilizations beginning at 3200 BC (along with the Babel-like pyramids). This information is not accurate according to God's Word. The worldwide Flood that destroyed everything on the earth began in 2348 BC, so none of these civilizations could have existed before then. It was only after the dispersion at Babel that these early civilizations started, as family groups began to spread around the world.

Some skeptics will also try to discount the account of the Tower of Babel by refusing to believe that the ancient people were skilled enough to accomplish such a task. According to God's Word, however, the people of antiquity were very intelligent. Genesis gives us insight into these people and what they were capable of. For instance, they were building cities (Genesis 4:17), they were raising and caring for livestock (Genesis 4:20), they made and played musical instruments (Genesis 4:21), and they were metalworkers in bronze and iron (Genesis 4:22). They were certainly talented enough (and sinful enough) to build this tower as a tribute to themselves and their own accomplishments—ignoring their Creator God and His instructions.

Be aware that information like the above is what all of us see and hear from the world—and it contradicts the Bible. It confuses and denies the infallibility of God's Word. We must continue to rely on the biblical worldview we know to be true.

HISTORICAL BACKGROUND

We see from the Genesis account that the people disobeyed God and built a tower and a city to make a name for themselves (Genesis 11:4). God confused the language, and the people dispersed throughout the earth (Genesis 11:8). This occurred a little more than 100 years after the Flood subsided in the year 2349 BC. Our understanding of history continues to confirm the biblical account of the Tower of Babel.

It is generally agreed that the Tower of Babel was a ziggurat temple-tower. This conclusion is based not on having discovered the Tower of Babel—which has not been found—but on discoveries of very similar "ziggurat" structures in other areas of the Middle East and beyond. The Egyptian pyramids in particular and, much later, the great Mayan temples of Central America are examples of this structure being spread around the globe from Babel.

Historically, we know that these ancient ziggurats were built to offer homage to the false gods of the people who built them. These structures are part of the idolatrous worship of these various people groups. We can connect this to our understanding that the building of the Tower of Babel was dishonoring of the one true God who spared Noah and his family and commanded them to be fruitful and multiply and fill the earth (Genesis 9:1).

Again, looking biblically at this entire account, we see that the dates given for these archaeological finds are inaccurate. We know, according to Scripture, that the Flood was about 4,300 years ago—and everything on the face of the earth was destroyed. Consequently, all evidences of civilization that we find have to be dated later than the Flood.

As the people dispersed from the plain of Shinar, they recalled their attempt to build the Tower of Babel and make a name for themselves. Thus, because men are wicked and, when left to their own devices will always turn from God, they once again began to build their cities and temples throughout the earth—the ziggurats that we find today.

For more information on this topic, see the Online Resource Page.

# Studying God's Word

Were the pyramids in Egypt built before the Tower of Babel?

Take notes as you study the following passages.

Genesis 11:1–9

Genesis 10:8–12

Genesis 10:25

 ## God's Word in the Real World

1. Were God's plans for the people to multiply and fill the earth thwarted by the disobedience of the people?

2. What attributes of God does this judgment of the people by confusing their languages demonstrate?

3. Does it surprise you that this rebellion happened so quickly—just a few generations after the Flood? Explain.

4. Knowing that this is the tendency of mankind, how do we conduct our lives so that we don't fall into this pattern?

5. How is this judgment at Babel a picture of God's continuing grace to mankind today, including you?

Prayer Requests

7

One Blood, One Race

Key Passages

- Genesis 10:1–32; 1 Samuel 16:7; Acts 17:26–27

What You Will Learn

- That all people are descendants of Adam and are of one blood.
- How the different people groups came to be.
- The connection between cavemen and the Tower of Babel.

Lesson Overview

After Babel, men spread throughout the world. These people may have moved into caves to survive. Different characteristics arose in different people groups, but all people are one race—from one blood—descendants of Adam and Eve.

Memory Verse

Acts 17:26–27 And He has made from one blood every nation of men to dwell on all the face of the earth, and has determined their preappointed times and the boundaries of their dwellings, so that they should seek the Lord, in the hope that they might grope for Him and find Him, though He is not far from each one of us.

📖 Prepare to Learn

SCRIPTURAL BACKGROUND

The Bible refers to all of us as being from one blood (Acts 17:26). God makes it abundantly clear that all humans are related, descendants of the first man, Adam (1 Corinthians 15:45), who was created in the image of God (Genesis 1:26–27). After the judgment of the Flood about 4,300 years ago, only Noah and his family remained, and from Noah's three sons—Shem, Ham, and Japheth—the world was repopulated (Genesis 9:18–19). But due to man's disobedience, God's judgment came once again at the Tower of Babel where He confused their language and caused them to spread out (Genesis 11:7–8).

According to God's Word, we are all related (Acts 17:26), we are all created in God's image (Genesis 1:26), and we are all sinners in need of salvation (Romans 3:23). This should convince us that God's plan was to promote unity among the human race—not an attitude of prejudice or racism.

Jesus instructed us to "Love your neighbor as yourself" (Matthew 22:39) and God tells us that "the Lord does not see as man sees; for man looks at the outward appearance, but the Lord looks at the heart" (1 Samuel 16:7). This is a biblical principle we must model and teach our children from an early age. We must avoid judging people because of their outward appearance, their ethnic features, or their disabilities. We are all one race—the human race. Our recognition of this fact will help to eliminate the prejudice and racism that permeates much of our culture today.

APOLOGETICS BACKGROUND

It is because of what happened at Babel that the world doesn't have a common language. We know of over 6,900 spoken languages in the world today. Yet it is likely that fewer than 100 languages emerged from the Tower of Babel when God confused their language. The languages that resulted from Babel are what we call "root" languages or language families. These root languages would have changed rapidly as they borrowed from other languages, developed new terms and phrases, and lost words. The biblical account of Babel occurred just as it is recorded. People of one common language have developed into people of thousands of languages.

The most controversy surrounding the Tower of Babel arises around the idea that we are all one race—the human race. Many people refuse to believe this biblical truth because of the major differences in appearance among the different people groups, such as skin color, hair, and eye shape.

Since skin color is such an obvious difference, let's look at that. The truth is, we all have the same skin pigment, melanin, just more or less of it. Lots of pigment is called *black*, and a little pigment is called *white*. We all have varying degrees of this pigment, creating differing shades of one basic color—brown.

The study of DNA and genetic makeup conducted by the Human Genome Project supports the biblical teaching that there is only *one* biological race of humans. The study determined that the differences in us that we perceive as so dramatic are a result of only a small fraction of our genes. In other words, we are all extremely similar in our genetic makeup. And what about those things that make us look different? They are very insignificant when taken into perspective.

HISTORICAL BACKGROUND

From a historical perspective, we know, according to Scripture, that the Flood occurred in 2349 BC—about 4300 years ago—and everything on the face of the earth was destroyed. The dispersion of the people at the Tower of Babel, around 2242 BC, marked the beginning of the spreading of civilization over the entire world. Consequently, when we study ancient history, we need to remember that evidences of civilization that we find have to be dated after 2242 BC.

Another historical consideration in our discussion of the dispersion of the people at Babel centers on what we hear about "primitive cavemen." These cavemen are often presented as animal-like by evolutionists to legitimize the ape-to-man development theory. They are often described as having lived thousands of years before civilizations like Egypt or Babylon. However, we know according to Scripture that they were the people God dispersed from Babel. They were not primitive but extremely skilled—enough so to be building cities (Genesis 4:17), raising and caring for livestock (Genesis 4:20), playing musical instruments (Genesis 4:21), and working in various metals (Genesis 4:22).

Although as a community they were accomplished at many things, once they were scattered, their survival depended on their individual skills alone. This may have resulted in some of the groups resorting to more primitive ways of surviving—they just didn't have all the skills they needed. And, the fact that they made their homes in caves proved their intelligence, as caves provide protection and shelter from the weather, animals, or enemies. These people—these so-called "primitive cavemen"—were no such thing. They were intelligent people making up intelligent families. They were not sub-human, but descendants of Adam and Eve just as we are.

For more information on this topic, see the Online Resource Page.

 Studying God's Word

Who in this room is your relative?

Take notes as you study the following passage.

Genesis 10:1–5

Grandsons of Noah

Fill out the Grandsons of Noah worksheet as you move through the lesson.

Take notes as you study the following passages.

Genesis 10:6–20

Genesis 10:21–32

Genesis 8:20–9:3

Mapping the Nations

Fill out the Mapping the Nations worksheet in small groups.

Take notes as you study the following passages.

Acts 17:26

Genesis 3:20

God's Word in the Real World

1. In 1 Samuel 16:7, when the eldest son Eliab came before
    Samuel, how did Samuel evaluate whether he would make
    a good king? How does this idea of judging based on our
    appearance relate to our topic today?

2. Why is this type of prejudice unbiblical?

3. Does God see any group of people differently with respect to their sin?

4. In Revelation 5:9, where have the people worshipping Christ been redeemed from?

5. What attitudes concerning people who are different from you do you need to repent of?

Prayer Requests

8
Job's Suffering

Key Passages

- Job 1:1–2:10, 31:5, 38:1–42:16; James 5:11; Romans 8:28–30

What You Will Learn

- That God is sovereign over every circumstance.

- The source of the faith and trust of Job.

- How the trials in our lives relate to God's plans for us.

Lesson Overview

The account of Job proclaims the sovereignty and omnipotence of God over all things—both good and bad. Job's faith and trust in God remained firm through much affliction. We can find comfort in knowing that, if we are children of God, He works everything in our lives according to His good purpose.

Memory Verse

Acts 17:26–27 And He has made from one blood every nation of men to dwell on all the face of the earth, and has determined their preappointed times and the boundaries of their dwellings, so that they should seek the Lord, in the hope that they might grope for Him and find Him, though He is not far from each one of us.

Prepare to Learn

SCRIPTURAL BACKGROUND

"Then the Lord said to Satan, 'Have you considered my servant Job, that there is none like him on the earth, a blameless and upright man, one who fears God and shuns evil?'" (Job 1:8). Thus begins this epic account of God's blameless servant turned over to the devices of Satan by God Himself. Oh, the sovereignty of God! It is too deep for any human to grasp—yet it is the very power that upholds all things in the universe (Hebrews 1:3).

God's sovereignty is the theme of the book of Job. The book opens allowing us a glimpse into the relationship between God and Satan. God controls Satan and uses him to accomplish His purposes on the earth. Satan can do only what God allows him to do—and in this account, God allowed Satan to test Job (Job 1:6, 1:8, 1:12, 2:6).

Job quickly discovered through his messengers that in one day he had lost his livestock, servants, and children (Job 1:13–19). And what a lesson we can learn from Job's faithful response as he tears his robe, shaves his head, falls to the ground, and worships the one who has taken every blessing from him in one day (Job 1:20). His worship and prayer in this desperate time provide a solid example of steadfast trust in the sovereign, almighty hand of God.

"Naked I came from my mother's womb, and naked shall I return there. The Lord gave, and the Lord has taken away; blessed be the name of the Lord" (Job 1:21).

God was not finished with Job yet, and He permitted Satan to again afflict Job—this time in his body and health (Job 2:7). With grace that could only come from God Himself, Job stood true to His Creator as he responded to his wife who suggested Job curse God and die (Job 2:9). Job plainly understood God's sovereignty as he asked her, "Shall we indeed accept good from God, and shall we not accept adversity?" (Job 2:10).

Job's friends approached to comfort him, but they only served to confound him with their accusations that it was because of his iniquity against God that he was suffering in this way (Job 4:7–8). They insisted that if Job would only repent of his sins, God would remove his suffering (Job 11:13–19). But if he refused to repent and continued in his wickedness, he would die (Job 11:20).

In chapter 19, we find Job clinging in his suffering and despair to the one thing he knew for sure—that his Redeemer lives! How Job yearned for what his heart knew to be true—that he would one day behold the Redeemer God with his very eyes (Job 19:25–27). Within the midst of this long Old Testament book, God gives us a foreshadowing of the Redeemer, Jesus Christ, and the gospel of forgiveness and redemption He would provide.

Job's suffering and the accusations of his friends continued. And finally, Job begged that the Almighty would answer him and reveal the purpose, wisdom, and reason behind his pain. In answer to Job's question, the Lord began a tirade of rhetorical questions— questions meant to humble Job by the demonstration of God's power, wisdom, knowledge, and greatness (Job 38–41).

In the end, God did not intend to answer Job's questions about the purpose of his suffering, but meant to draw Job's focus to Himself—the sovereign Ruler, Creator, and Sustainer of the entire universe. Job learned his lesson well when he answered the Lord by saying, "I know that you can do everything, and that no purpose of yours can be withheld from You" (Job 42:2).

Our God is in control. We know that all things work together for good to those who love God (Romans 8:28); that our God is in heaven and does all that He pleases (Psalm 115:3); that He works all things according to the counsel of His will (Ephesians 1:11); and that no one speaks and it will come to pass unless the Lord has commanded it. Both woe and well-being proceed from the mouth of the Most High (Lamentations 3:37–38).

APOLOGETICS BACKGROUND

Throughout this account Job continued to argue his innocence, and his friends continued to tell him he must be guilty because bad things don't happen to good people. This is a very popular misconception even today, and one that Jesus's disciples held to, but one that Jesus flatly rejected (see John 9:1–3; Luke 13:1–5).

Many today insist that a loving God would not let innocent people suffer. They have no concept of their own sinfulness, nor do they understand the holiness of God—that He can't tolerate any disobedience against Him. Instead, these people make a god in their imaginations to suit their own desires and reject what the Bible clearly teaches—there are no innocent people (Ecclesiastes 7:20); all of mankind has sinned (Romans 3:23); and the wages of sin is death (Romans 6:23).

But is the suffering we experience on earth the direct result of our sin? Is the suffering a manifestation of God's punishment? Scripture tells us that God disciplines His children. However, this discipline is exhibited out of the Lord's love for us—we are not perfect, and consequently we need training from our heavenly Father (Hebrews 12:5–7). Paul also explains that our suffering may be a consequence of a sinful decision, choice, or lifestyle—God is not mocked by our rebellion; we will reap what we sow (Galatians 6:7–8); our suffering and trials often test our faith and produce patience (James 1:3); we can be humbled by affliction brought on by God (2 Corinthians 12:7); and often our trials give us the wisdom and understanding to comfort others in their troubles (2 Corinthians 1:3).

We often will not be given a clear answer as to why we are suffering—just as Job's question was never answered by God. However, we must remember that God is our sovereign, holy God and He is able to work all things together for good for those who are called according to His purpose (Romans 8:28). His desire for His children is not to necessarily make us happy—but to make us holy (1 Peter 1:15) while conforming us throughout our lives to the image of His own Son, our Lord and Savior Jesus Christ (Romans 8:29).

HISTORICAL BACKGROUND

The book of Job has often been praised as a masterpiece of literature.

Victor Hugo wrote, "Tomorrow, if all literature was to be destroyed and it was left to me to retain one work only, I should save Job." Alfred Lord Tennyson called Job "the greatest poem, whether of ancient or modern literature." Daniel Webster said that "the Book of Job taken as a mere work of literary genius is one of the most wonderful productions of any age or of any language." And Martin Luther said that this book is "more magnificent and sublime than any other book of Scripture."

When was the book of Job written and who is its author? Except for the first eleven chapters of Genesis, the book of Job is probably the oldest book in the Bible. Most likely, Job himself was the original author (Job 19:23–24), writing down an account of his life after the restoration of his health and prosperity. He probably lived around the time of Abraham, and because there is no mention of the laws given by Moses or even of Israel—it is believed he definitely lived before Jacob.

Job was considered "the greatest of all the men of the East" (Job 1:3) and he "dwelt as a king in the army" (Job 29:25). Job lived in the land of Uz, which is believed to be the land of Edom (see Lamentations 4:21). Uz, who perhaps settled there first, was a grandson of Shem (Genesis 10:22–23).

Job is not a fictional character in a great dramatic poem, as many have suggested. He was a real man who served a real God, and as James said, a man who persevered and experienced the compassion and mercy of God: "You have heard of the perseverance of Job and seen the end intended by the Lord—that the Lord is very compassionate and merciful" (James 5:11).

For more information on this topic, see the Online Resource Page.

 Studying God's Word

Do good things happen to good people?

Take notes as you study the following passages.

Job 1:1–5

Job 1:6–12

Job 1:13–22

Job 2:1–6

Job 2:7–10

Job 38:1–42:16

James 5:11

Romans 8:28–30

 ## Understanding Trials

For each of the questions below, write a sentence or two that explains your thinking on the topic in light of the ideas we explored in Job.

1. Have you heard it said before that "good things happen to good people"? How does this statement compare to what you have just read about Job's trials?

2. It is certainly true that sin has consequences, but is it biblically accurate to say that every trial you face is the result of sin in your life? Why or why not?

3. Identify a time in your life when your sin caused you to suffer consequences. Read Hebrews 12:5–11. How does this passage help you understand God's role and purpose in that situation?

4. Considering the following attributes of God, describe how each of these can lead you to look to God in times of suffering:

Wise –

Loving –

Omniscient –

Sovereign –

5. In the middle of Job's lament he says:

> For I know that my Redeemer lives,
> And He shall stand at last on the earth;
> And after my skin is destroyed, this I know,
> That in my flesh I shall see God,
> Whom I shall see for myself,
> And my eyes shall behold, and not another.
> How my heart yearns within me!
> Job 19:25–27

How can trials in your life point you to the hope that you have in Christ and a future in heaven?

 ## God's Word in the Real World

1. How would you respond to someone who made the claim that trials in your life or an illness you are facing is the result of sin you have not repented of?

2. Some people would claim that Job was not a real person, but simply a character in a poem that helps us understand suffering. How could James 5:11 be used to correct this misunderstanding?

3. What comfort can we draw from the behind-the-scenes look at the authority God exercises over Satan's actions?

4. How does a Romans 8:28 view of circumstances differ from those who believe in ideas like karma, fate, chance, or the general principle that what goes around comes around?

5. What idea have you drawn from our lesson today that you can put into practice as you face various trials throughout the next week?

Prayer Requests

9
God Calls Abram

Key Passages

- Genesis 11:27–12:9; Hebrews 11:8–16

What You Will Learn

- How Abram demonstrated his faith in God.
- The difference between rewards on earth and rewards in heaven.

Lesson Overview

God called Abram to leave his family and his father's house. God promised Abram that he would have a great land, a great nation, and a great name and that he would be a blessing. Abram believed God and demonstrated amazing faith and obedience even though he never saw the nation promised by God. We learn in Hebrews that because of his faith, Abram was confident in the heavenly rewards he had not seen.

Memory Verse

Acts 17:26–27 And He has made from one blood every nation of men to dwell on all the face of the earth, and has determined their preappointed times and the boundaries of their dwellings, so that they should seek the Lord, in the hope that they might grope for Him and find Him, though He is not far from each one of us.

SCRIPTURAL BACKGROUND

Before the creation of the world God determined to reveal Himself through His merciful plan of redemption (Matthew 25:34; Ephesians 1:4). God offers this plan by grace through faith (Ephesians 2:8) and originally revealed it to Adam and Eve in the Garden of Eden. In the midst of the Curse that came as a result of their disobedience, God gave the promise of a Redeemer who would crush the serpent's head (Genesis 3:15).

As we learn of God's call to Abram (later renamed *Abraham*), we see more of the promise whose fulfillment is revealed throughout Scripture. God's eternal plan to bring redemption continued with the Abrahamic Covenant—God would make Abraham a great nation that would in turn bless all nations (Genesis 12:1–3). Abraham was called physically to be the father of the Jewish nation; but more than that, he was called to be the father of all those who believe by faith in the promised Messiah, both Jew and Gentile (Romans 4:9–12).

It was because of Abraham's amazing faith—faith in things hoped for but not yet seen (Hebrews 11:1)—that he could obediently follow God's lead and believe the incredible promises made to him (Genesis 17:17). In fact, his faith provided the stamina for him to leave his home, go to a foreign country, and wait for his wife Sarah to conceive and bear a child. This was the child that would produce for Abraham descendants as many as the stars of the sky and as innumerable as the sand by the sea (Hebrews 11:8–12). These descendants would become a new nation, appointed by God Himself, through which He would ultimately bring a Savior, Jesus Christ (Matthew 1:1).

As mentioned earlier, our faith comes through grace, as a gift from God. In Romans 4, the Apostle Paul presents Abraham as an example of faith. Abraham proved his faith by his obedience. He did not waver at the promise of God through unbelief, but was strengthened in faith (Romans 4:20). This faith was what provided Abraham's righteousness (Romans 4:22), just as it is our faith in God's provided Savior, Jesus, that brings us to a righteous standing before Him (2 Corinthians 5:21).

APOLOGETICS BACKGROUND

We trust the Bible as the inerrant Word of God and stand on it soundly as our authority in all things. But it is exciting when God allows us to confirm biblical accounts with present-day discoveries as He has done for us in this account. You see, the ancient city of Ur (Abram's birthplace as mentioned in Genesis 11) was rediscovered and excavated by archaeologists between 1922 and 1934, providing much more information about the city and life during the time of Abram (Genesis 11:28).

The people of Ur had adopted Nanna-Sin, the moon god, as their patron. A ziggurat was erected as a temple to Nanna-Sin, perhaps hearkening back only a few generations to the Tower of Babel, when God judged the people for disobedience and idolatry by confusing their language. Ur was a thoroughly pagan city where the religious leaders and rulers used their idolatry to control the populace. Royal burial pits were discovered that included masters and their servants—giving the appearance that once the royalty died, servants willingly (or unwillingly) committed suicide. In one case, as many as 68 servants were found buried with their master.

After realizing the pagan, godless nature of the people of Ur, we are not surprised that God would call Abram to move from that city and journey to a new location where He would continue the fulfillment of His plan of redemption for all who would believe.

HISTORICAL BACKGROUND

What better way is there to look at the history of Abraham than to consider the genealogy carefully recorded by God? Genesis begins at the beginning and gives us details of the history of mankind—starting with Adam. (See Genesis chapters 10 and 11.)

These genealogies are God's way of revealing His intention from the very beginning to use sinful man to accomplish His perfect plan of redemption. We witness generations of the descendants of Adam weaving through history to the patriarch Abraham. We recognize his role in the plan and watch expectantly as he begets Isaac to carry on the seed that will one day provide the Messiah.

The history of this account includes God's call to Abram to leave Ur and go to the land of Canaan. Abram was traveling with his father and family (Genesis 11:31) and stopped short of Canaan in Haran (Acts 7:2–3). We aren't told why this caravan stopped in Haran, but we do know that Abram's father, Terah, succumbed to the idolatry of that pagan city (Joshua 24:2). It was after Terah died in Haran that God again called Abram to the land of Canaan (Genesis 12:1). Once Abram arrived in Canaan, the Lord appeared to him and promised the land to his descendants.

Here again we observe the faith of Abram as he built an altar to the Lord and worshipped Him despite the fact that he was still childless. Abram believed God and knew that the truth and promises yet to be fulfilled in this land would include all mankind for all eternity.

For more information on this topic, see the Online Resource Page.

 # Studying God's Word

How does God reward faith and obedience?

_____

_____

_____

Take notes as you study the following passages.

Genesis 11:27–12:9

_____

_____

_____

Hebrews 11:8–16

_____

_____

_____

 # A Heavenly Hope

Working in small groups, answer the questions below.

1. From Hebrews 11:1, write a biblical definition for faith.

2. Below is a list of events in Abraham's life that demonstrate his faith through his obedience to God. Some of these will be discussed in later lessons and some we have discussed today. Next to each item, try to identify a similar situation in your life in which you have demonstrated or may someday demonstrate your faith.

Leaving his home and family for an unknown country

Building an altar to worship God

Offering Lot the choice of land to live in

Waiting for a son to fulfill God's promise

Offering Isaac, the son of promise, as a sacrifice

3. How does Abraham embody the instructions in Colossians 3:1–5?

4. What things have you set your hope on here on earth?

5. What would need to change about your lifestyle if you were to act as a "stranger and pilgrim" here on this earth?

6. If we are going to trust God to fulfill His promises, why is an understanding of God's faithfulness important?

God's Word in the Real World

1. We know that God has promised to reward those who place their faith in Him. When can we expect to receive those rewards?

2. Have you ever heard the expression "you are so heavenly minded that you are no earthly good"? Is this a biblically grounded idea in light of what we have been studying today?

3. Why is it so important to understand God's attribute of faithfulness as we seek to follow Jesus?

4. How does the world react to the idea of storing up treasures in heaven rather than seeking to build fortunes and seek pleasures here on earth?

5. In what ways are you failing to set your mind on things above? How can you seek to change this attitude?

6. As you seek to live your life with a focus on heavenly things, how will you be viewed by unbelievers?

Prayer Requests

_____

_____

_____

_____

10
God's Covenant with Abram

Key Passages

- Genesis 15:1–21, 17:1–27; Galatians 3:15–18

What You Will Learn

- The nature of the covenant between God and Abraham.

- How the descendants of Abraham connect to the hope of the gospel.

Lesson Overview

God made a covenant with Abram, which was ultimately fulfilled through Jesus Christ—a descendant of Abram through Isaac. Jesus Christ is the promised descendant through whom all nations have been blessed. He alone brings the hope of redemption to the world.

Memory Verse

Acts 17:26–27 And He has made from one blood every nation of men to dwell on all the face of the earth, and has determined their preappointed times and the boundaries of their dwellings, so that they should seek the Lord, in the hope that they might grope for Him and find Him, though He is not far from each one of us.

Prepare to Learn

SCRIPTURAL BACKGROUND

Before the beginning of time God established a plan to redeem a people to Himself (Genesis 3:15). According to God's plan this people would descend from His servant Abram. Abram would not only be the physical father of the Israelites (Genesis 12:2) but would also serve as the spiritual father of all who would come to faith in Jesus Christ (Romans 4:11). Throughout these chapters in Genesis, God's promise to Abram and his descendants—the Abrahamic Covenant—is given, confirmed, and amplified. The covenant begins in Genesis 12:1–3, where Abram is promised:

- God will make him a great nation (Genesis 12:2).

- God will bless him (Genesis 12:2).

- He will be a blessing (Genesis 12:2).

- God will bless those who bless Abram (Genesis 12:3).

- God will curse those who curse Abram (Genesis 12:3).

- Through Abram all nations will be blessed (Genesis 12:3).

But Abram is childless. How will this promise ever come to pass? His question is finally voiced in Genesis 15:2: "Lord God, what will you give me, seeing I go childless?" God's response? "Look now toward heaven, and count the stars . . . . So shall your descendants be" (Genesis 15:5).

God was faithful to His promises as He continued to shape Abram's life to His purposes. Chapter 17 revealed God again confirming this covenant made between God and Abram and his descendants (Genesis 17:7). The sign of the covenant was to be circumcision (Genesis 17:10). And it is here that God changes his name—from Abram, meaning *exalted father*, to Abraham, meaning *father of a multitude* (Genesis 17:5). Even in this name change we see God reassuring Abraham of His faithfulness.

Throughout this amazing saga and in spite of apparently impossible circumstances, we know that Abraham "believed in the Lord, and He accounted it to him for righteousness" (Genesis 15:6). In fact, we see these words repeated throughout the New Testament (Romans 4:3, 4:22; Galatians 3:6; James 2:23) as a reminder that it is not our works of obedience but faith in God— the belief in what He says—that leads to righteousness.

APOLOGETICS BACKGROUND

More and more we are confronted by a culture that refuses to believe that the Bible is God's inerrant Word. Though these people rarely read or study the Word of God themselves, we are often able to present them with historical information and recent findings.

For example, as God described the land Abraham was soon to overcome and inhabit, He mentioned the Hittite people (Genesis 15:19–21). Many skeptics had discounted the accuracy of the Bible and the history of the Old Testament because of the lack of extra-biblical historical information about the Hittites. Archaeologists in 1832 confirmed God's Word when they discovered a city that proved to be the capital of the Hittite empire, Hattusa, at modern-day Boghazköy in Turkey. Now the Hittites are accepted as a once-great civilization, and God has silenced those who would doubt Him in this matter.

At one time skeptics even questioned God's Word because of His statement to Abraham that his descendants would outnumber the stars of the heaven and be as numerous as the sands of the sea (Genesis 22:17). It was thought that no more than 10,000 stars existed. They did not appear to be as numerous as the sand on the seashore and certainly not more than we could count. But with the invention of powerful telescopes, today we can actually estimate the number of stars, and we know that in our galaxy alone there are over 100 billion stars.

With the reliability of the Bible increasingly under attack, it's encouraging to observe God using science and archaeology, not as enemies of His truth, but as confirmation that His Word—every word—proves true (Proverbs 30:5–6).

HISTORICAL BACKGROUND

It was much more dramatic than a simple handshake. It was a sacred sign that a covenant had been made. It seems strange that God would request a three-year-old heifer, a three-year-old female goat, a three-year-old ram, a turtledove, and a young pigeon after Abram questioned Him about the land he was to inherit (Genesis 15:7–9).

But this was the requirement of some ancient covenants. A promise between two individuals sometimes involved cutting animals in half and placing them on either side of a pathway. The pledging parties would walk between the freshly killed animals as a sign of the curse they were willing to accept—if they reneged on their agreement, may they too be cut limb from limb just as these animals had been (see Jeremiah 34:18–20).

The covenant with Abram was not a typical ancient covenant; it included the God of Israel. God caused Abram to fall into a deep sleep, and after dark, a smoking oven and a burning torch passed between the animal pieces (Genesis 15:17). While Abram slept, God Himself, represented by the oven and the torch, bound Himself solemnly to His promise. God alone made the commitment because God alone could fulfill it. His promises to Abraham would indeed be kept.

For more information on this topic, see the Online Resource Page.

 **Studying God's Word**

How is Jesus connected to Abraham?

Take notes as you study the following passages.

Genesis 15:1–21

Genesis 17:15–27

 Abraham's Seed

Working in small groups, answer the questions below.

1. Read the following passages and look for two common threads. Record them in the space below. Romans 4:1–5:2; Galatians 3:1–18

2. Looking at the Galatians passage above, what does Paul clarify about the Seed promised to Abraham? (This is a reference to Genesis 22:18.)

3. God promised Abraham that all of the nations of the world would be blessed through him (Genesis 12:3). Knowing that Jesus is the Seed of Abraham, how have the nations of the world been blessed in Him?

4. Was Abraham a sinful man?

5. Was Abraham counted righteous because of his works?

6. Is any person ever counted as righteous because of their works?

7. What is the connection between faith and righteousness?

8. If Abraham was saved, his sins must have been covered. How was Jesus involved in Abraham's righteousness?

9. How is your hope of salvation in Christ different from Abraham's?

God's Word in the Real World

1. What truth from the Scriptures we looked at today has helped you see God's grace in the account of Abraham?

2. How has your view of earning righteousness changed in light of the passages we have looked at today?

3. If you have received Christ's forgiveness, how does knowing that God is unchanging and absolutely faithful give you peace and assurance of your salvation?

4. As you share the gospel with others, you will likely encounter people who claim that they are good people and that God will accept them based on all the good things they have done. How could you use Abraham to help them understand the error of their thinking?

 # Prayer Requests

11
Sodom and Gomorrah

Key Passages

- Genesis 18:1–33, 19:1–29

What You Will Learn

- That God's justice demands a punishment for sin.
- The sins that God hates.
- How God shows mercy toward sinners.

Lesson Overview

The Lord and two angels appear to Abraham and announce judgment on Sodom and Gomorrah because of the sin and wickedness God sees there. Abraham pleads not only for the cities but for his nephew Lot. God must punish sin, but He has mercy on Lot and his family.

Memory Verse

Acts 17:26–27 And He has made from one blood every nation of men to dwell on all the face of the earth, and has determined their preappointed times and the boundaries of their dwellings, so that they should seek the Lord, in the hope that they might grope for Him and find Him, though He is not far from each one of us.

📖 Prepare to Learn

SCRIPTURAL BACKGROUND

The journey of Abram to Canaan is one wrought with detours and adventure. The Lord told Abram to leave the land of his family and settle in a land the Lord would show him. Abram was to be the head of a great nation, a blessing to many, and his name would be great (Genesis 12:1–3). Abram listened and obeyed and left the land of Ur. God tells us that Lot, Abram's nephew, was part of the company of travelers from the beginning of the journey. After settling first in Haran (Genesis 11:31), they proceeded at the Lord's call to Canaan. Then there was another detour to Egypt because of a famine (Genesis 12:10). Through all of their wanderings, the Lord continued to increase their livestock and the land they traversed was no longer efficient to support Abram, Lot, and all of their possessions (Genesis 13:5–7). This is when uncle and nephew parted ways. Abram to the land of Canaan and Lot to the cities of the plain—where sin and wickedness prevailed against the Lord (Genesis 13:12–13).

God's justice demands punishment for sin and wickedness, and He was soon to providentially bring an end to the sin that permeated Sodom and Gomorrah. In a meeting between Abraham, the Angel of the Lord (Jesus), and two angels, the Lord confirmed that Abraham and Sarah would bear a son (Genesis 18:14). He also revealed the plan to destroy the wickedness of Sodom and Gomorrah (Genesis 18:20–21).

Abraham pleaded with the Lord to spare the city. However, God must punish sin; His justice demands that He punish those who turn from Him in wickedness. And there were fewer than ten righteous in the city (Genesis 18:32). This account illustrates just how wicked men can be. Lot, too, had succumbed to the evil influence of the city as demonstrated when he offered his own daughters to the men of the city to satisfy their lusts and protect the angels (Genesis 19:6–8).

But God is also merciful. And His mercy was shown to Lot and his daughters. In spite of their own sinfulness, they were spared from the destruction of the city (Genesis 19:16).

This account is tragic. The sin of man is great and God's judgment is to be feared—and not taken lightly. Lot's wife did not learn that lesson. And it was only moments after she was mercifully spared death in the city that she again blatantly disobeyed God during the escape—when she looked back at the destruction behind her (Genesis 19:17). For this she was judged and turned into a pillar of salt (Genesis 19:26).

The terrible destruction of Sodom and Gomorrah is an event

referred to throughout Scripture to demonstrate the severity of God's judgment: Deuteronomy 29:23; Isaiah 1:9, 13:19; Jeremiah 50:40; Lamentations 4:6; Amos 4:11; Zephaniah 2:9; Matthew 10:15; Mark 6:11; Luke 17:28–29; Romans 9:29; 2 Peter 2:6; Jude 1:7.

And yet God also revealed His mercy—by sparing Lot and his daughters. This is the mercy He provides to all sinners who in faith and repentance accept His forgiveness and turn to Jesus Christ.

APOLOGETICS BACKGROUND

There are many who cannot believe that this account could possibly be true. What can we say to those blinded to the truth? First of all, the fact that this event is referenced so many times throughout Scripture (see above for list) verifies that there was never any doubt by these writers that this event occurred just as it was recorded.

We know that those who do not rely on the authority of God's Word resort to relying on man's "evidence." And there was no historical or archaeological evidence to corroborate the biblical account—until recently.

It is clear from various biblical passages that Sodom and Gomorrah should be located in the Dead Sea region. When Abraham and his nephew Lot parted ways (Genesis 13:8–13), Lot chose to settle in the Jordan valley "in the direction of Zoar" and moved his tents to "the cities of the plain" as far as Sodom. According to Genesis 14, the cities of the plain, which include Sodom, Gomorrah, Zoar, Zeboiim, and Admah, joined forces to battle a coalition of Mesopotamian kings in the "Valley of Siddim" (Genesis 14:8)—that is, the Salt Sea. This is referring to the Dead Sea region.

Between 1973 and 1979 two archaeologists surveyed an area southeast of the Dead Sea and located the remains of five cities. From north to south the cities are Bab Edh-Dhra (first discovered in 1924), Numeira, Safi, Feifa, and Khanazir. Could these be the five "cities of the plain" identified in Genesis?

The most remarkable feature of Bab Edh-Dhra is the number of graves. An estimated 20,000 tombs are located on the site. These family tombs held approximately half a million people with over three million pottery vessels. This was clearly a well-populated area in the past, and may well be the ancient city of Sodom.

The excavation of the city of Numeira exposed that this entire area was covered by the ashy debris of its final destruction, up to 16 inches in depth. This, coupled with the fact that the Arabic name for this city has similar consonants as the Hebrew name for Gomorrah, led biblical archaeologists to conclude that this could be the city of Gomorrah.

"Proof" is not necessary to verify God's Word. In fact, we need nothing more than the word of the one who ordained and accomplished this historical account. However, God allows for these confirmations so that we will be better equipped to defend our faith and the Bible against the skeptics who attempt to dishonor and discredit it.

HISTORICAL BACKGROUND

The biblical narratives of this time period in terms of customs, laws, legal agreements, and family arrangements fit well with what we know from historical records left by other societies of the Middle East, such as the Amorites, Sumerians, and Akkadians.

During this particular period in history in the Middle East, the role of the patriarch in family life was very important. Family structure included three levels: tribe, family, and household (Joshua 7:14). The fundamental societal unit of the household included a patriarch, his wife, his sons and their wives, his grandchildren, and other dependents. These households often lived in a compound, with houses around a central courtyard, encircled by a low wall.

Abraham, as patriarch of his household, was responsible for the economic support, religious well-being, and safety of his entire household (Genesis 14:13–16). In Genesis 18 we see Abraham, as the patriarch, fulfilling his hospitality obligations to protect and care for sojourners or aliens, too (Leviticus 19:33–34). Hospitality was one of the most highly regarded virtues of the ancient world, and still is in many societies of the Middle East. Abraham showed his guests great honor by preparing them a meal.

Again, as we compare the history book of the universe with secular historical accounts, we gain confirmation and confidence that God's Word is true.

For more information on this topic, see the Online Resource Page.

 Studying God's Word

How can God be both just and merciful?

_____

_____

_____

Take notes as you study the following passages.

Genesis 18

_____

_____

Genesis 19

_____

_____

 Respectable Sins

Read the passages below and consider your own personal understanding of the nature of sin.

1. Read 1 Corinthians 6:9–10. Looking at this list of sins, do you typically think of thieves in the same category as adulterers or homosexuals? What about adultery compared to homosexuality?

    Does this passage make a distinction between people who commit these sins?

Which of these sins have you been guilty of? (Consider that looking with lust is the same as adultery [Matthew 5:28] and theft is theft regardless of the value of the object.)

2. Read Ephesians 5:3–6. Which of these sins are tolerated by many Christians?

   What is the penalty for each of these sins in verses 5 and 6?

   Does the text make a distinction between these sins?

Later this week, read the following passages and continue to reflect on your understanding of sin and your relationship with God.

3. Read 1 Corinthians 6:9–11. What very important idea, for a Christian, is introduced in verse 11? What hope does this give you?

4. Read Ephesians 5:1–13. What allows Christians to walk in love? Is this true in your life?

5. Read Romans 5:6–10. How does this passage give you hope in Christ?

God's Word in the Real World

1. Abraham and Sarah both laughed at the idea of having a child in their old age despite God's clear promise to them. How does knowing that God was faithful to His promise to them encourage you in your walk before the Lord?

2. How does God's promise of the Seed of Abraham, Jesus, demonstrate His mercy?

3. If you were sharing the gospel with someone who claims to be homosexual, how could you use 1 Corinthians 6:9–11 to minimize some of the strong emotional reaction that comes with this issue?

4. Many people object that eternal punishment of hell is not appropriate for the little sins that people commit on earth. Why is it just that any sin against God, from a lie to murder, is worthy of such strong punishment?

5. Using the analogy of a criminal standing before a judge, how can we help others understand that God is both merciful and just?

Prayer Requests

12
Abraham and Isaac

Key Passages

- Genesis 22:1–19; John 1:29–34;
  Hebrews 11:17–19

What You Will Learn

- How Abraham demonstrated his faith and trust in God.

- How the sacrifice of Isaac and the ram compares to the sacrifice of Christ on the Cross.

- The promise of the Messiah through history.

Lesson Overview

God called Abraham to offer Isaac, the son of promise, as a sacrifice. Abraham acted in faith, obeyed God, and continued to trust His promise. In the end, God provided a ram in Isaac's place. We see in this account a foreshadowing of Christ and the salvation God promises through Him.

Memory Verse

Acts 17:26–27 And He has made from one blood every nation of men to dwell on all the face of the earth, and has determined their preappointed times and the boundaries of their dwellings, so that they should seek the Lord, in the hope that they might grope for Him and find Him, though He is not far from each one of us.

📖 Prepare to Learn

SCRIPTURAL BACKGROUND

"And the Lord visited Sarah as He had said, and the Lord did for Sarah as He had spoken" (Genesis 21:1). With this, God kept His promise of a son to Abraham and Sarah and fulfilled the covenant and promise previously made to Abraham (Genesis 17:7). This was the child of promise. It was through his seed that the line of the Messiah would come.

Abraham was one hundred years old when Isaac was born (Genesis 21:5). And he celebrated the birth of this long-awaited son (Genesis 21:8). But this celebration would quickly turn somber.

Genesis 22 records one of the most moving accounts in the Old Testament. For God now determined in His wisdom to test the faith of Abraham. Did Abraham truly believe the promises of God? Where did Abraham's allegiance lie? Was Abraham willing to trust and obey the one true God?

"Take now your son, your only son Isaac, whom you love, and go to the land of Moriah, and offer him there as a burnt offering on one of the mountains of which I shall tell you" (Genesis 22:2). How heartbreaking this must have been. Yet Abraham, demonstrating his complete confidence in God, saddled his donkey, took his son, his servants, and the wood for the burnt offering, and began his journey (Genesis 22:3).

The faith and obedience shown by Abraham is seldom seen more vividly. He demonstrated it when he spoke to his servants, "the lad and I will go yonder and worship, and come back to you" (Genesis 22:5). This statement—that they would come back—revealed that Abraham believed God would keep His word and if necessary, bring his son back to life (Hebrews 11:17–19). Again he exhibited amazing faith when, as the trip neared its conclusion, Isaac wondered to his father, "where is the lamb for a burnt offering?" (Genesis 22:7). "God will provide for Himself the lamb" (Genesis 22:8). Abraham was fully prepared to obey and offer his son, but it also appears that somehow he knew the principle of substitutionary sacrifice—and that is where his hope was. Perhaps he had heard the record of Adam's sin and how God covered their nakedness and shame with the skins of the dead animals in the garden.

On the mountaintop the moment came: Isaac on the altar built by his own father; Abraham with hand stretched out to present to God the ultimate act of obedience (the death of this precious son promised so long ago) (Genesis 22:9–10); then the Angel of the Lord calling, "Do not lay your hand on the lad, or do anything to him; for now I know that you fear God, since you have not withheld your son, your only son, from me" (Genesis 22:12). Abraham had passed the test. His trust was absolute; his obedience complete. And God provided a ram for the sacrifice (Genesis 22:13). Here the Angel of the Lord confirmed again the Abrahamic Covenant—the land, the descendants, and the blessings that would be fulfilled through Abraham (Genesis 22:15–18).

How blessed we are to see in this historical account a clear foreshadowing of the perfect sacrifice, provided by God Himself, Jesus Christ, the Lamb slain from the foundation of the world (Revelation 13:8). "The Lamb of God who takes away the sins of the world" (John 1:29)! He alone is worthy to receive power and riches and wisdom and strength and honor and glory and blessing (Revelation 5:12)! He is the only one able to offer hope and forgiveness for eternity to all who will sincerely repent of their sins and turn to Him in total trust and obedience.

APOLOGETICS BACKGROUND

As we consider the amazing display of obedience in Abraham and the merciful intervention of our holy God, we also see God's omniscience and sovereignty as He weaves His plan of redemption in Jesus Christ throughout all of Scripture. This account of Abraham and Isaac is just one such example.

When God called Abraham to Mount Moriah, He knew exactly what would occur in this sacred place in the future. Years later, in this same region, God would appear to David and stop the plague that would beset Israel in retribution for David's disobedience against God (1 Chronicles 21:14–15). Later, near this mountain, David's son Solomon would build the house of the Lord (2 Chronicles 3:1) where the Most Holy Place would allow limited access by the High Priest—once a year—into God's presence (Leviticus 16:2). And then, in the culmination of God's eternal plan, Jesus Christ Himself would be offered near this place as the perfect sacrifice and final atonement for the sins of everyone who would believe.

The significance of this demands reverence to our all-knowing God. For on this mountain, where God provided a ram for Isaac as his sacrifice—God also provided the only Lamb whose blood is able to ransom a people to God from every tribe and tongue and people and nation (Revelation 5:9).

On that fateful day, the day of Christ's death, the temple curtain that separated the people from their God was torn. The barrier between God and man had been removed forever. No longer would access to our holy God be limited. But believers can now enter boldly into the Holy of Holies by the blood of Jesus our High Priest. We can draw near with a true heart in full assurance of faith, knowing our hearts and bodies are washed with pure water (Hebrews 10:19–22).

HISTORICAL BACKGROUND

We know that the actual Abrahamic Covenant included Abraham leaving his family and his home and journeying to a place the Lord would show him. God also promised a great nation, a great name, and many blessings (Genesis 12:1–2). The culmination of this covenant would be the birth of Jesus Christ—a descendant of Abraham—the one through whom all nations would be blessed (Genesis 18:18).

However, this covenant was foreshadowed at the very beginning—in the Garden of Eden. Even as God was pronouncing the curse, He was also offering the hope of victory over death and sin. "And I will put enmity between you and the woman, and between your seed and her Seed; He shall bruise your head, and you shall bruise His heel" (Genesis 3:15). Below is a brief glimpse of the history of this amazing covenant:

- Genesis 3:15 God promised a Redeemer in the Garden of Eden

- Genesis 12:1–3 God presented His covenant to Abram

- Genesis 12:4–5 Abram and his family began their journey

- Genesis 17:1–27 God changed Abram's name to Abraham and promised him a son

- Genesis 26:3–5 God confirmed the Abrahamic covenant to Abraham's son—Isaac

- Genesis 28:13–15 God confirmed the Abrahamic covenant to Isaac's descendant—Jacob

- Genesis 45:7–8 God preserved the people of Israel and led them to Egypt through Jacob's descendant—Joseph

- Genesis 49:10 The Messiah was promised through another of Jacob's descendants—Judah

- 1 Chronicles 2:1–15 King David descended from the tribe of Judah

- 2 Samuel 7:1–17 The Davidic Covenant was established—the line of David would rule forever

- Luke 1:31–33 Jesus will receive the throne of David and will reign over the house of Jacob forever

Do you see God's faithfulness . . . His omniscience . . . His mercy . . . His grace . . . His sovereignty through this historical account encompassing thousands of years and woven perfectly throughout the history of the world? We serve an awesome God. For of Him and through Him and to Him are all things to whom be glory forever (Romans 11:36)!

For more information on this topic, see the Online Resource Page.

 Studying God's Word

How does Isaac represent Jesus Christ?

Take notes as you study the following passages.

Genesis 22:1–19

Hebrews 11:17–19

From the Seed to the Lamb

Complete the From the Seed to the Lamb worksheet.

Write the connections between Isaac and Christ represented by these Scripture passages:

Matthew 1:19–23

John 3:16–18

John 19:17–18

Ephesians 5:1–2

Isaiah 53:10

John 1:29–34

1 Corinthians 15:3–4

2 Chronicles 3:1

 # God's Word in the Real World

1. What can you take from today's lesson to help you be assured of God's faithfulness to His promises?

2. What benefit do you see in tracing the promise of a Savior, as we did in the cross-referencing activity, throughout the entire Bible?

3. Some of you may have been asking yourselves if you could have been as faithful as Abraham in his situation. If you ever doubt your ability, how can you find assurance that your faith will carry you through?

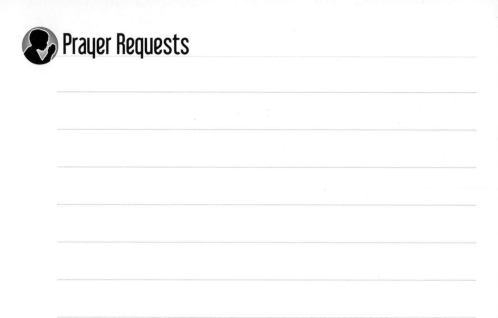

Prayer Requests

13
The Ice Age

Key Passages

- Genesis 8:20–22; Romans 1:20

What You Will Learn

- The connection between the Flood and the Ice Age.

- How God's attributes are displayed in the uniformity of His creation.

Lesson Overview

Although the Bible does not directly speak of it, the physical evidence on the earth's surface supports a period of time when ice covered a large portion of the Northern and Southern Hemispheres. The global Flood of Noah's day would have created the proper conditions for the Ice Age. We can apply our God-given reason to develop scientific explanations for how the evidence can be understood.

Memory Verse

Acts 17:26–27 And He has made from one blood every nation of men to dwell on all the face of the earth, and has determined their preappointed times and the boundaries of their dwellings, so that they should seek the Lord, in the hope that they might grope for Him and find Him, though He is not far from each one of us.

📖 Prepare to Learn

SCRIPTURAL BACKGROUND

It has often been said that the Bible is not a science textbook. That is true in the sense that the Bible does not describe scientific details, such as that of genetic inheritance. However, the Bible is not silent on topics of scientific interest. One area that seems to get little attention in Scripture is the occurrence of an ice age. In fact, very little in the Bible would directly connect to the idea of an ice age. But this doesn't mean that an ice age did not occur or that it is an unbiblical idea.

As we try to develop scientific descriptions to explain the physical evidence around us, we must always remember that the Bible must be the authority that we check everything against. The Flood provides a major historical point that we must first understand before forming any ideas about the occurrence of an ice age. Since the Flood was global, it would have removed the evidence for any ice age that occurred before the Flood. So, as we develop models to explain the evidence, they should explain the Ice Age after the Flood, since the earth contains abundant evidence for an Ice Age. (As a significant event, we capitalize Ice Age to differentiate it from the general idea of ice ages.)

After the Flood, God promised Noah and all of his descendants that the world they lived in would never be completely flooded again. In that same passage, God also promised that He would continue to uphold the earth in a relatively constant manner. The seasons, day and night, and cycles of hot and cold would continue under God's control until the end of the earth (Genesis 8:20–22).

If you search for the word *ice* in your concordance, you will find only three references, all in the book of Job (Job 6:16, 37:10, 38:29 NKJV). Job lived about 200 years after the Flood, and the references to the freezing of broad waters could refer to the Ice Age. In general, we wouldn't expect to hear a lot about major snow storms in the Bible since it was written primarily within a subtropical climate. Snow was certainly known to the biblical writers, and it often gets used in Scripture as a metaphor for pure whiteness or purity. One of the most striking passages comes as God tells Isaiah that his sins of scarlet can be made as white as snow (Isaiah 1:18). What a wonderful promise we have through Christ and the gospel.

APOLOGETICS BACKGROUND

From a secular perspective, there have been many ice ages spanning millions of years. The most recent reached its maximum about 20,000 years ago, and the small ice sheets and pockets of glaciers are the remnants of that period.

From a biblical perspective, there is no reason to doubt that much of the earth was covered in ice sheets for a period of time. The physical evidence is consistent with a recent time where the advancing ice sheets carved the earth's surface, leaving moraine valleys, kettle lakes, and other features characteristic of glaciation.

The events of the Flood can explain the Ice Age in a way that no other model from secular or biblical scientists can match. As the fountains of the great deep broke open, they would have released lava and hot water into the ocean. Clouds and ash would have filled the atmosphere as the continents shifted. The atmosphere would have been cooled as sunlight was reflected away from the earth, leading to a cooler climate over the continents.

This mixture of warm oceans with increased evaporation and cool climates caused massive amounts of snow to fall. The snow continued to accumulate into ice sheets that covered large portions of North America, Europe, and Asia in the Northern Hemisphere. Computer simulations of the conditions provided by the Flood support these ideas and are superior to models based on secular assumptions. As the oceans cooled and the atmosphere cleared, the snow decreased. The Ice Age reached its maximum approximately 500 years after the Flood and melted significantly within the next 200 years.

Unlike the frozen tundra that now exists in much of Siberia, Alaska, and Canada, these areas once supported communities of mammoths, giant beavers, antelope, and grasses. As the Ice Age ended and the climate shifted, giant storms covered some mammoths in sediments and trapped others on islands. The food supply decreased, and the animals either moved south or died of starvation. Today, we find their remains buried in the permafrost layer—some are amazingly well-preserved.

In terms of global warming, the earth has been warming gradually ever since the peak of the Ice Age (glacial maximum). Those temperatures have surely fluctuated, including the Little Ice Age from 1300 to 1880, but temperatures generally are on the rise. But this doesn't mean that man is causing the warming or that the rise is a bad thing. God promised to maintain the earth through cycles of hot and cold, day and night, and we can trust that promise (Genesis 8:20–22). However, we do not have cause to exploit the earth for our selfish reasons; rather, we are to act as stewards of God's good gifts to us.

As creation scientists continue to study these issues, they will refine models and resolve problems that exist today. Not unlike the secular models, much more research is needed and many more questions remain to be answered. However, when we use the Bible as the starting point for looking at the evidence, we can trust that we can better understand how God has worked in His creation.

HISTORICAL BACKGROUND

The secular view of multiple ice ages happening over millions of years does not make sense in light of the earth's biblical history. Even the most recent ice age in the secular view would have occurred many thousands of years before God created the universe. This gives us a solid reason for rejecting such an interpretation of history. As we survey the biblical timeline, the Flood occurred about 4,300 years ago, so the Ice Age must have occurred more recently than that.

This also corresponds to the writing of the book of Job, in which we see references to ice and snow, specifically the freezing of broad stretches of water. The current models show the Ice Age peaking within a few hundred years after the Flood's end. This places the Ice Age during the time of the dispersion from Babel.

As people were spreading to the north, they would have encountered ice sheets encroaching into Europe and Asia. Many of the cave-dwelling cultures would have lived in these areas and hunted animals like mammoths, mastodons, wooly rhinos, giant deer, and others that are often depicted on the walls of the caves people used as shelter.

Another opportunity that resulted from the Ice Age was the creation of land bridges. As the water evaporated from the oceans, areas like the Bering Strait would have been passable. As people moved across Asia, they would have been able to travel to Alaska over dry land. Similarly, people could have passed from Indonesia into Australia aboard boats traveling relatively short distances.

Another recent area of research is the existence of large cities that have been found underwater off of the coast. If the water level had been lower, cities built along the coast during the period of the Ice Age would have been flooded as the ice sheets melted and the sea level rose. Regardless of what evidence we uncover, we must always strive to honor God and His Word as we seek to understand the world we live in and the past events that have shaped it.

For more information on this topic, see the Online Resource Page.

 ## Studying God's Word

How many ice ages have there been?

Take notes as you study the following passage.

Genesis 8:20–22

 ## The Ice Age Video Notes

Take notes as you view The Ice Age video clips.

 ## God's Word in the Real World

1. How might the Ice Age be a part of discussions about the truth of the gospel?

2. Is it important for each of you to know the details and inner workings of the latest Ice Age models as you seek to share the gospel with others? Why or why not?

3. How could you respond to someone who asks you a question about the Ice Age, or any other topic, that you are unable to answer?

4. Many people are afraid of the effects of global warming. How does Genesis 8:20–22 give you assurance of the future?

Prayer Requests